ECLIPSES

ABDO
Publishing Company

A Buddy Book **by Marcia Zappa**

Buddy BOOKS
The Universe

VISIT US AT
www.abdopublishing.com

Published by ABDO Publishing Company, 8000 West 78th Street, Edina, Minnesota 55439.

Printed in the United States of America, North Mankato, Minnesota.
102010
012011
♻ PRINTED ON RECYCLED PAPER

Coordinating Series Editor: Rochelle Baltzer
Contributing Editors: Megan M. Gunderson, BreAnn Rumsch, Sarah Tieck
Graphic Design: Maria Hosley
Cover Photograph: *Photo Researchers, Inc.*: Detlev van Ravenswaay.
Interior Photographs/Illustrations: Barcroft/Frame (p. 8); *NASA*: Eclipse Predictions by Fred Espenak, NASA's GSFC (p. 15); *Photo Library* (p. 23), *Photo Researchers, Inc.*: John Chumack (pp. 11, 12), Detlev van Ravenswaay (pp. 5, 7, 9, 19), Sheila Terry (p. 25), Frank Zullo (p. 7); *Shutterstock*: Daniel Hebert (p. 28), Rob Marmion (p. 30), oorka (p. 27), Detelina Petkova (p. 27), razihusin (p. 29), Alexy Stiop (p. 16), worldswildlifewonders (p. 27).

Library of Congress Cataloging-in-Publication Data

Zappa, Marcia, 1985-
  Eclipses / Marcia Zappa.
    p. cm. -- (The universe)
  ISBN 978-1-61714-688-6
  1. Eclipses--Juvenile literature. I. Title.
  QB175.Z37 2011
  523.9'9--dc22
                              2010029670

Table Of Contents

What Is an Eclipse?

Space is full of interesting objects. The moon, the stars, and the planets shine brightly in the night sky.

Many interesting events also take place in space. One type of event is an eclipse. This happens when one space object moves into the shadow of another.

Eclipses create unusual and beautiful scenes.

5

A Closer Look

Eclipses can happen to any space object. But, common eclipses seen from Earth are of the sun and the moon. These occur as Earth **orbits** the sun and the moon orbits Earth.

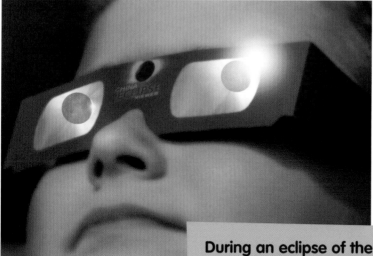

During an eclipse of the sun, sunlight is very powerful. People must use special tools to view one safely. These include eclipse viewing glasses (*above*) and projections (*below*).

Good-bye Sun

An eclipse of the sun is called a solar eclipse. During this event, the moon moves between the sun and Earth. It casts a shadow on Earth. From Earth, the sun seems to darken.

During some solar eclipses, the sun's outer atmosphere shows. This is called the corona.

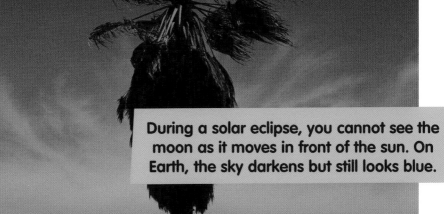

During a solar eclipse, you cannot see the moon as it moves in front of the sun. On Earth, the sky darkens but still looks blue.

Part or Whole

There are three kinds of solar eclipses. A partial solar eclipse happens when the moon blocks part of the sun. During a total solar eclipse, the moon blocks the whole sun.

Partial Solar Eclipse

Total Solar Eclipse

Sun

Moon

Earth

On Earth, people in the purple area see a total solar eclipse. People in the blue area see a partial solar eclipse.

An annular solar eclipse is when the moon blocks the sun's center. This happens because the **orbits** of Earth and the moon are oval shaped. This causes the distance between Earth, the moon, and the sun to change.

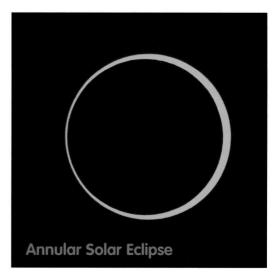

Annular Solar Eclipse

During an annular eclipse, the moon is farthest from Earth. And, Earth is closest to the sun.

When this happens, the moon's shadow cannot reach Earth. So, the moon never hides the whole sun.

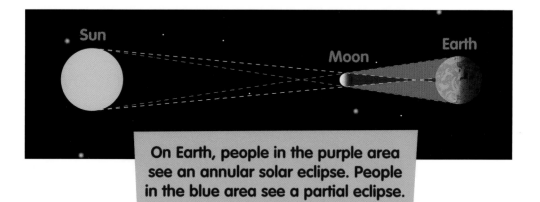

On Earth, people in the purple area see an annular solar eclipse. People in the blue area see a partial eclipse.

Moving Right Along

An eclipse of the sun can only be seen from certain spots on Earth. This is because the moon's shadow is small compared to Earth's surface.

As Earth spins, the moon's shadow moves across its surface. During a total solar eclipse, the shadow's path is called the path of totality.

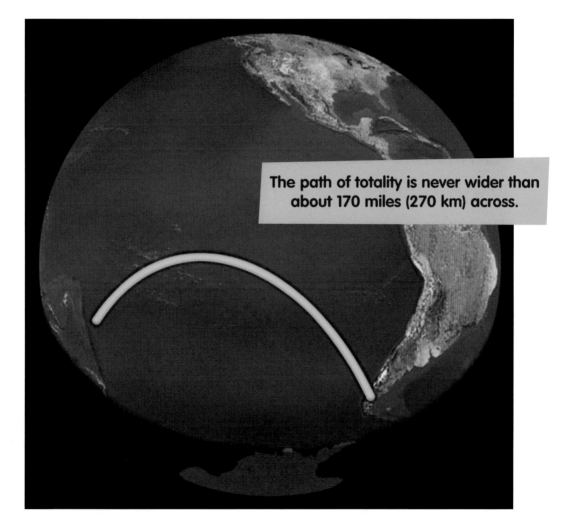

The path of totality is never wider than about 170 miles (270 km) across.

Hidden Moon

An eclipse of the moon is called a lunar eclipse. During this event, the moon moves into Earth's shadow. Earth blocks the sun's direct light from reaching the moon.

Our view of the moon changes as it moves into and out of Earth's shadow.

There are two main kinds of lunar eclipses. A partial lunar eclipse happens when part of the moon moves into Earth's shadow. A total lunar eclipse happens when the whole moon moves into Earth's shadow.

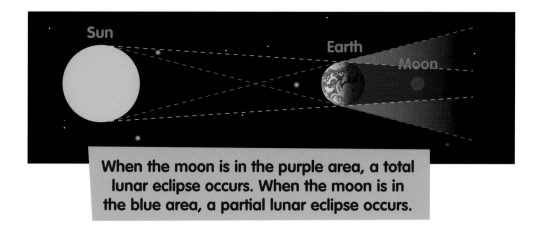

When the moon is in the purple area, a total lunar eclipse occurs. When the moon is in the blue area, a partial lunar eclipse occurs.

The moon doesn't usually disappear during a lunar eclipse. Instead, it often appears reddish.

Earth's **atmosphere** causes this. It makes the sun's light bend. And, gases, dust, and clouds **filter** the light. This makes it look reddish as it shines on the moon.

When lunar eclipses occur, they can be
seen at night in most areas on Earth.

Once in a While

During an eclipse, Earth, the moon, and the sun form a straight line. This doesn't happen often. And, total eclipses are very uncommon.

The moon's **orbit** around Earth **tilts** away from Earth's orbit around the sun. So, Earth's shadow does not often fall on the moon. And, the moon's shadow does not often hit Earth.

Earth, the moon, and the sun line up a few times each year. This causes at least two solar eclipses and up to three lunar eclipses each year.

Sun

Earth

Moon

21

Discovering Eclipses

People have been interested in eclipses for thousands of years. Ancient Chinese people believed solar eclipses were caused by a dragon trying to eat the sun.

Historians think the story of the dragon may be more than 4,000 years old!

Over the years, scientists learned to **predict** eclipses. So around 1850, they began traveling to see uncommon solar eclipses. When they returned, they shared what they had seen.

Early scientists used telescopes to study lunar eclipses. These tools allowed them to view faraway objects.

25

Studying Eclipses

Scientists have learned a lot about space by studying eclipses. They have also learned more about the sun and the moon. Eclipses have even taught them about light.

Around 1940, an eclipse showed scientists that the moon is covered in dust.

Studying eclipses teaches scientists about the sun's corona.

Eclipses have helped scientists prove that light bends as it passes a large space object.

27

Animals notice solar eclipses. As it grows dark, animals that are normally active at night start coming out. Animals that are normally active during the day become quiet. They start getting ready for bed!

Owls are usually active at night. But, they may come out during solar eclipses!

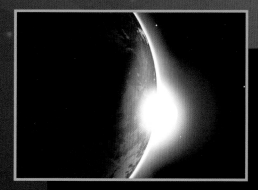

During a lunar eclipse, **astronauts** on the moon would see a solar eclipse. From their view, Earth would block the sun.

The next total solar eclipse to be seen from the United States will be in 2017.

On average, a total solar eclipse lasts only about two and a half minutes. A total lunar eclipse can last more than one and a half hours!

Voyage to Tomorrow

Today, scientists can almost exactly **predict** eclipses. This allows them to be ready with cameras and other tools. Some scientists even post live videos of eclipses on the Internet.

On the Internet, people can watch eclipses take place around the world.

Important Words

astronaut a person who is trained for space travel.

atmosphere (AT-muh-sfihr) the layer of gases that surrounds a space object.

filter to act as a filter. A filter is something that draws in and traps some types of light. This changes the color of the light.

orbit the path of a space object as it moves around another space object. To orbit is to follow this path.

predict to say something is going to happen before it does.

tilt to be positioned at a slope or an angle.

Web Sites

To learn more about **eclipses** visit ABDO Publishing Company online. Web sites about **eclipses** are featured on our Book Links page. These links are routinely monitored and updated to provide the most current information available.

www.abdopublishing.com

INDEX